This Book belongs to:

....

Thank you for choosing this coloring book!
Please consider leaving a positive review on
Amazon. It would mean a lot to me and help
other customers find the book.
Your feedback is greatly appreciated!

⭐⭐⭐⭐⭐

💚 **Get Free Printable Coloring Pages** 💚
& Join Our Community!

https://linktr.ee/5ideas.publishing

- MAXIMUS PRIME -

THANK YOU!

THANK YOU FOR CHOOSING US
TRY OUR OTHER COLORING BOOKS ON AMAZON
- MAXIMUS PRIME COLORING BOOKS-

ARTWORK 1

0 = White

1 = Black

2 = Dark Blue

3 = Sky Blue

4 = Light Blue

5 = Cream

6 = Violet

7 = Dark Orange

8 = Medium Blue

9 = Dark Grey

10 = Dark Brown

11 = Tan

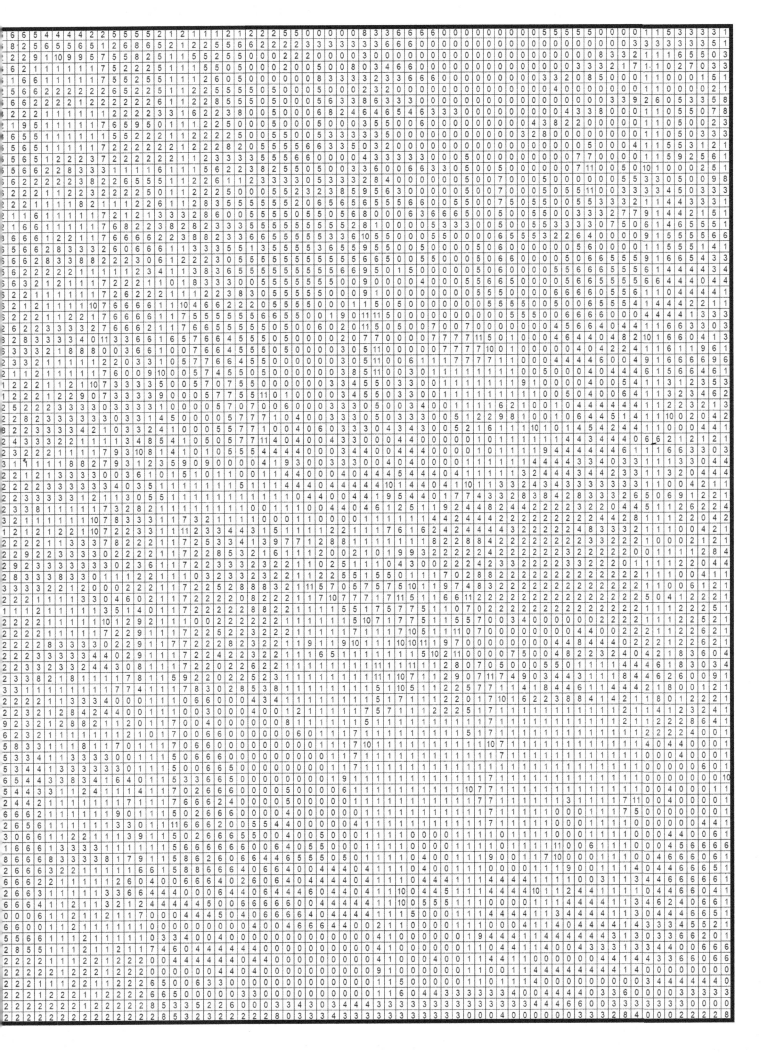

ARTWORK 2

0 = Dark Blue

1 = White

2 = Black

3 = Dark Red

4 = Light Blue

5 = Red

6 = Tan

7 = Sky Blue

8 = Dark Orange

9 = Light Brown

10 = Dark Brown

11 = Light Orange

TIP: USE THE SUGGESTED COLOR PALETTE ON THE BACK COVER FOR YOUR REFERENCE.

ARTWORK 3

0 = Black

1 = Dark Brown

2 = White

3 = Dark Red

4 = Dark Orange

5 = Medium Blue

6 = Red

7 = Light Orange

8 = Tan

9 = Cream

10 = Sky Blue

11 = Light Blue

ARTWORK 4

0 = Black

1 = Dark Red

2 = White

3 = Dark Blue

4 = Violet

5 = Tan

6 = Dark Orange

7 = Light Brown

8 = Red

9 = Medium Green

10 = Dark Brown

TIP: USE THE SUGGESTED COLOR PALETTE ON THE BACK COVER
FOR YOUR REFERENCE.

- MAXIMUS PRIME COLRING BOOK-

ARTWORK 5

0 = Black

1 = Bright Green

2 = Dark Green

3 = Red

4 = Dark Red

5 = Dark Brown

6 = White

7 = Tan

8 = Light Orange

9 = Dark Orange

TIP: USE THE SUGGESTED COLOR PALETTE ON THE BACK COVER
FOR YOUR REFERENCE.

- MAXIMUS PRIME COLRING BOOK-

ARTWORK 6

0 = Black

1 = Dark Grey

2 = Dark Red

3 = Dark Orange

4 = Cream

5 = White

6 = Light Grey

7 = Tan

8 = Red

9 = Dark Brown

10 = Light Brown

TIP: USE THE SUGGESTED COLOR PALETTE ON THE BACK COVER
FOR YOUR REFERENCE.

- MAXIMUS PRIME COLRING BOOK-

ARTWORK 7

0 = Black

1 = Medium Blue

2 = Sky Blue

3 = Light Grey

4 = Light Blue

5 = Dark Blue

6 = White

7 = Dark Brown

8 = Dark Red

9 = Dark Orange

10 = Light Orange

11 = Red

12 = Yellow

TIP: USE THE SUGGESTED COLOR PALETTE ON THE BACK COVER
FOR YOUR REFERENCE.

- MAXIMUS PRIME COLRING BOOK-

ARTWORK 8

0 = Black

1 = Dark Green

2 = Dark Grey

3 = Dark Red

4 = White

5 = Bright Green

6 = Dark Orange

7 = Yellow Green

8 = Red

9 = Light Brown

10 = Yellow

11 = Dark Brown

12 = Light Orange

TIP: USE THE SUGGESTED COLOR PALETTE ON THE BACK COVER
FOR YOUR REFERENCE.

- MAXIMUS PRIME COLRING BOOK-

ARTWORK 9

0 = Black

1 = White

2 = Medium Blue

3 = Cream

4 = Dark Grey

5 = Red

6 = Tan

7 = Light Blue

8 = Dark Red

9 = Sky Blue

10 = Light Brown

11 = Dark Brown

12 = Dark Orange

TIP: USE THE SUGGESTED COLOR PALETTE ON THE BACK COVER
FOR YOUR REFERENCE.

- MAXIMUS PRIME COLRING BOOK-

ARTWORK 10

0 = Sky Blue

1 = Red

2 = Dark Red

3 = White

4 = Black

5 = Light Grey

6 = Dark Grey

7 = Tan

8 = Light Brown

9 = Light Orange

10 = Dark Orange

11 = Dark Brown

12 = Dark Blue

TIP: USE THE SUGGESTED COLOR PALETTE ON THE BACK COVER
FOR YOUR REFERENCE.

ARTWORK 11

0 = Black

1 = Sky Blue

2 = Dark Blue

3 = Medium Blue

4 = White

5 = Light Blue

6 = Dark Brown

7 = Dark Red

8 = Tan

9 = Light Brown

10 = Dark Orange

11 = Light Orange

TIP: USE THE SUGGESTED COLOR PALETTE ON THE BACK COVER
FOR YOUR REFERENCE.

- MAXIMUS PRIME COLRING BOOK-

ARTWORK 12

0 = Medium Blue

1 = Sky Blue

2 = White

3 = Light Grey

4 = Light Blue

5 = Dark Blue

6 = Dark Red

7 = Dark Brown

8 = Light Orange

9 = Dark Grey

10 = Black

11 = Light Brown

12 = Dark Orange

13 = Red

ARTWORK 13

0 = Black

1 = White

2 = Light Grey

3 = Dark Red

4 = Dark Grey

5 = Light Brown

6 = Cream

7 = Dark Brown

8 = Dark Orange

9 = Dark Green

10 = Bright Green

11 = Red

12 = Yellow Green

13 = Light Orange

TIP: USE THE SUGGESTED COLOR PALETTE ON THE BACK COVER
FOR YOUR REFERENCE.

- MAXIMUS PRIME COLRING BOOK-

ARTWORK 14

0 = Black

1 = Red

2 = Light Orange

3 = Bright Green

4 = White

5 = Dark Green

6 = Medium Blue

7 = Sky Blue

8 = Dark Orange

9 = Dark Blue

10 = Dark Purple

11 = Dark Red

12 = Yellow Green

13 = Light Grey

14 = Violet

TIP: USE THE SUGGESTED COLOR PALETTE ON THE BACK COVER FOR YOUR REFERENCE.

ARTWORK 15

0 = Black

1 = White

2 = Yellow

3 = Bright Green

4 = Dark Green

5 = Yellow Green

6 = Red

7 = Sky Blue

8 = Dark Red

9 = Light Blue

10 = Light Orange

11 = Dark Orange

12 = Dark Purple

13 = Dark Pink

14 = Dark Brown

15 = Cream

16 = Medium Green

17 = Pink

TIP: USE THE SUGGESTED COLOR PALETTE ON THE BACK COVER
FOR YOUR REFERENCE.

- MAXIMUS PRIME COLRING BOOK-

ARTWORK 16

0 = Black

1 = White

2 = Sky Blue

3 = Medium Blue

4 = Light Blue

5 = Dark Blue

6 = Dark Red

7 = Violet

8 = Dark Brown

9 = Cream

10 = Red

11 = Light Brown

12 = Tan

13 = Dark Pink

14 = Pink

15 = Dark Orange

TIP: USE THE SUGGESTED COLOR PALETTE ON THE BACK COVER
FOR YOUR REFERENCE.

- MAXIMUS PRIME COLRING BOOK-

ARTWORK 17

0 = Dark Blue

1 = Black

2 = Medium Blue

3 = White

4 = Light Blue

5 = Sky Blue

6 = Dark Brown

7 = Violet

8 = Dark Grey

9 = Tan

10 = Cream

11 = Dark Red

12 = Dark Orange

13 = Light Brown

14 = Light Orange

TIP: USE THE SUGGESTED COLOR PALETTE ON THE BACK COVER
FOR YOUR REFERENCE.

- MAXIMUS PRIME COLRING BOOK-

ARTWORK 18

0 = Black

1 = Dark Green

2 = Dark Red

3 = Red

4 = White

5 = Bright Green

6 = Light Grey

7 = Dark Grey

8 = Yellow

9 = Light Orange

10 = Dark Brown

11 = Dark Orange

12 = Cream

13 = Medium Green

14 = Yellow Green

ARTWORK 19

0 = Black
1 = Medium Blue
2 = White
3 = Sky Blue
4 = Light Blue
5 = Dark Red
6 = Dark Orange
7 = Red
8 = Dark Brown
9 = Cream

ARTWORK 20

0 = Sky Blue

1 = White

2 = Black

3 = Dark Blue

4 = Light Blue

5 = Dark Red

6 = Medium Blue

7 = Tan

8 = Dark Orange

9 = Cream

10 = Light Brown

TIP: USE THE SUGGESTED COLOR PALETTE ON THE BACK COVER
FOR YOUR REFERENCE.

- MAXIMUS PRIME COLRING BOOK-

ARTWORK 21

0 = White

1 = Black

2 = Dark Red

3 = Light Blue

4 = Medium Blue

5 = Red

6 = Dark Blue

7 = Dark Orange

8 = Light Orange

TIP: USE THE SUGGESTED COLOR PALETTE ON THE BACK COVER
FOR YOUR REFERENCE.

- MAXIMUS PRIME COLRING BOOK-

ARTWORK 22

0 = Black

1 = Dark Green

2 = Red

3 = Bright Green

4 = Dark Red

5 = Yellow Green

6 = Yellow

7 = White

8 = Dark Pink

9 = Cream

10 = Light Orange

11 = Medium Green

TIP: USE THE SUGGESTED COLOR PALETTE ON THE BACK COVER
FOR YOUR REFERENCE.

- MAXIMUS PRIME COLRING BOOK-

ARTWORK 23

0 = Dark Blue

1 = Black

2 = Medium Blue

3 = White

4 = Sky Blue

5 = Light Blue

6 = Cream

7 = Tan

8 = Dark Brown

9 = Light Brown

10 = Dark Orange

11 = Light Orange

TIP: USE THE SUGGESTED COLOR PALETTE ON THE BACK COVER
FOR YOUR REFERENCE.

- MAXIMUS PRIME COLRING BOOK-

ARTWORK 24

0 = Black

1 = Dark Green

2 = Dark Red

3 = White

4 = Dark Orange

5 = Red

6 = Bright Green

7 = Light Grey

8 = Dark Grey

9 = Light Orange

10 = Yellow

11 = Medium Green

12 = Yellow Green

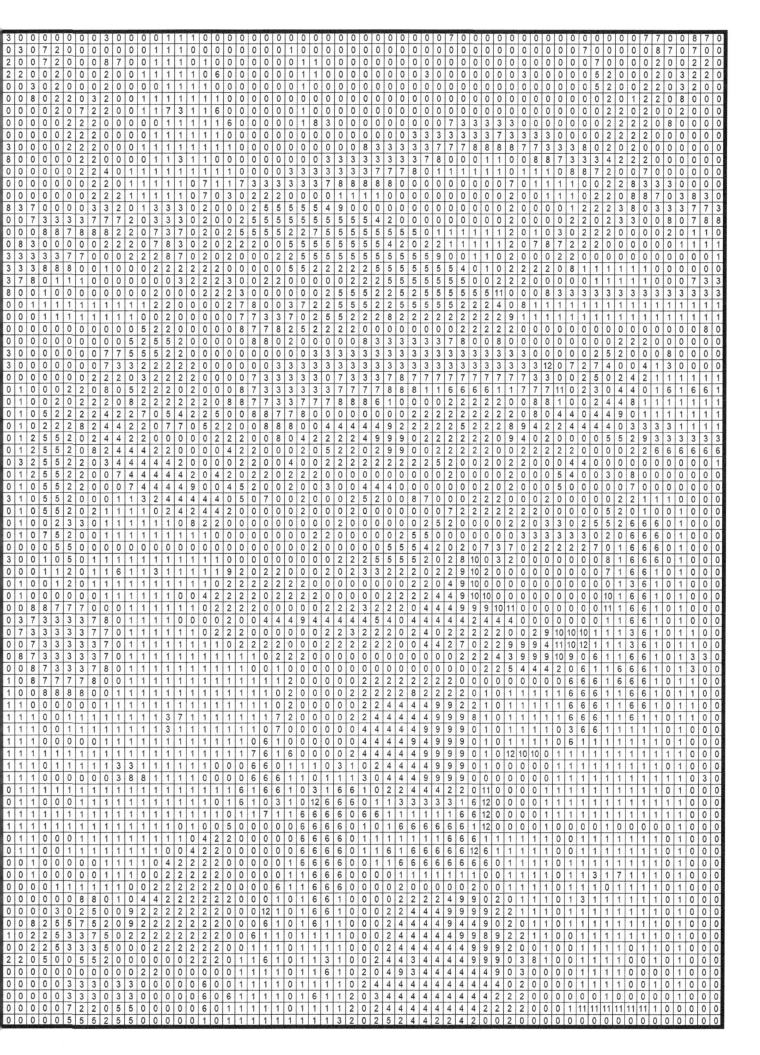

ARTWORK 25

0 = Black

1 = Dark Green

2 = White

3 = Red

4 = Light Grey

5 = Dark Red

6 = Dark Grey

7 = Bright Green

8 = Dark Orange

9 = Yellow Green

10 = Yellow

11 = Medium Green

ARTWORK 26

0 = Black

1 = Sky Blue

2 = Light Blue

3 = Red

4 = White

5 = Dark Red

6 = Bright Green

7 = Yellow Green

8 = Medium Blue

9 = Dark Green

10 = Yellow

11 = Medium Green

12 = Dark Pink

13 = Pink

14 = Dark Orange

15 = Light Orange

TIP: USE THE SUGGESTED COLOR PALETTE ON THE BACK COVER
FOR YOUR REFERENCE.

- MAXIMUS PRIME COLRING BOOK-

ARTWORK 27

0 = White

1 = Black

2 = Medium Blue

3 = Red

4 = Dark Red

5 = Light Grey

6 = Dark Grey

7 = Dark Orange

8 = Tan

9 = Dark Brown

10 = Light Brown

11 = Light Orange

12 = Cream

TIP: USE THE SUGGESTED COLOR PALETTE ON THE BACK COVER
FOR YOUR REFERENCE.

- MAXIMUS PRIME COLRING BOOK-

ARTWORK 28

0 = Black

1 = Dark Blue

2 = Sky Blue

3 = Medium Blue

4 = Dark Red

5 = White

6 = Light Blue

7 = Light Grey

8 = Dark Brown

9 = Pink

10 = Dark Pink

11 = Red

12 = Tan

13 = Light Brown

TIP: USE THE SUGGESTED COLOR PALETTE ON THE BACK COVER
FOR YOUR REFERENCE.

ARTWORK 29

0 = Black

1 = White

2 = Dark Red

3 = Medium Blue

4 = Cream

5 = Sky Blue

6 = Red

7 = Light Blue

8 = Dark Blue

9 = Dark Green

10 = Dark Orange

11 = Light Orange

12 = Bright Green

TIP: USE THE SUGGESTED COLOR PALETTE ON THE BACK COVER
FOR YOUR REFERENCE.

- MAXIMUS PRIME COLRING BOOK-

ARTWORK 30

0 = Black

1 = White

2 = Medium Blue

3 = Sky Blue

4 = Red

5 = Dark Red

6 = Light Blue

7 = Dark Orange

8 = Cream

9 = Light Grey

10 = Violet

11 = Dark Grey

12 = Tan

13 = Dark Brown

14 = Light Brown

15 = Light Orange

TIP: USE THE SUGGESTED COLOR PALETTE ON THE BACK COVER
FOR YOUR REFERENCE.

- MAXIMUS PRIME COLRING BOOK-

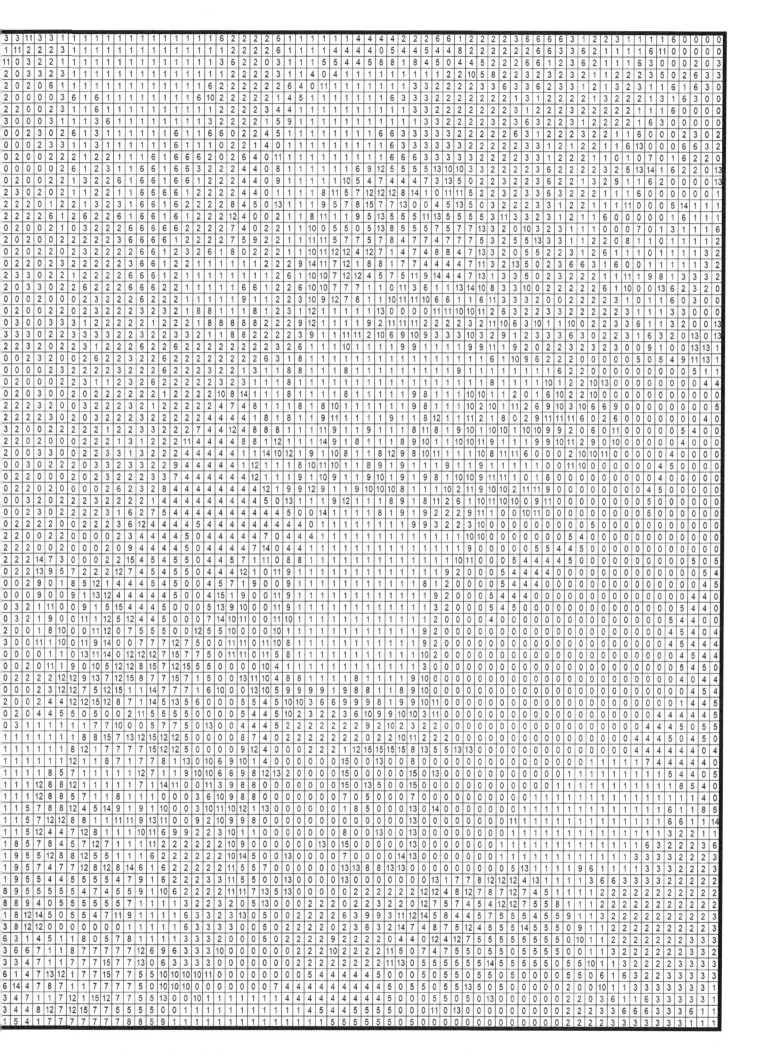

ARTWORK 31

0 = Black

1 = White

2 = Cream

3 = Dark Orange

4 = Dark Red

5 = Sky Blue

6 = Red

7 = Dark Green

8 = Light Orange

9 = Yellow

10 = Dark Grey

11 = Medium Blue

12 = Dark Blue

13 = Bright Green

14 = Dark Brown

15 = Yellow Green

16 = Medium Green

17 = Pink

TIP: USE THE SUGGESTED COLOR PALETTE ON THE BACK COVER
FOR YOUR REFERENCE.

- MAXIMUS PRIME COLRING BOOK-

ARTWORK 32

0 = Black

1 = Light Orange

2 = Red

3 = Sky Blue

4 = White

5 = Medium Blue

6 = Dark Brown

7 = Light Blue

8 = Dark Blue

9 = Dark Orange

10 = Bright Green

11 = Dark Purple

12 = Dark Pink

13 = Tan

14 = Dark Grey

15 = Yellow Green

16 = Violet

TIP: USE THE SUGGESTED COLOR PALETTE ON THE BACK COVER FOR YOUR REFERENCE.

- MAXIMUS PRIME COLRING BOOK-

ARTWORK 33

0 = Black

1 = Light Blue

2 = White

3 = Sky Blue

4 = Medium Blue

5 = Dark Brown

6 = Light Orange

7 = Dark Red

8 = Dark Orange

9 = Tan

10 = Light Brown

11 = Red

ARTWORK 34

0 = Dark Blue

1 = Black

2 = Dark Brown

3 = White

4 = Medium Blue

5 = Light Brown

6 = Light Blue

7 = Sky Blue

8 = Tan

9 = Cream

10 = Violet

11 = Dark Grey

12 = Red

13 = Dark Pink

14 = Dark Purple

TIP: USE THE SUGGESTED COLOR PALETTE ON THE BACK COVER
FOR YOUR REFERENCE.

- MAXIMUS PRIME COLRING BOOK-

ARTWORK 35

0 = Sky Blue

1 = Black

2 = Pink

3 = Light Blue

4 = Medium Blue

5 = Dark Blue

6 = Cream

7 = Dark Brown

8 = Dark Pink

9 = Light Brown

10 = White

11 = Dark Purple

12 = Tan

13 = Dark Red

14 = Red

TIP: USE THE SUGGESTED COLOR PALETTE ON THE BACK COVER
FOR YOUR REFERENCE.

ARTWORK 36

0 = Black

1 = White

2 = Dark Red

3 = Light Blue

4 = Sky Blue

5 = Dark Grey

6 = Dark Orange

7 = Dark Blue

8 = Medium Blue

9 = Light Orange

10 = Dark Purple

11 = Yellow Green

12 = Yellow

13 = Dark Brown

14 = Dark Pink

TIP: USE THE SUGGESTED COLOR PALETTE ON THE BACK COVER FOR YOUR REFERENCE.

ARTWORK 37

0 = Black

1 = Sky Blue

2 = Light Orange

3 = Dark Red

4 = White

5 = Red

6 = Yellow Green

7 = Dark Orange

8 = Yellow

9 = Medium Blue

10 = Dark Green

11 = Dark Pink

12 = Cream

13 = Medium Green

14 = Bright Green

15 = Violet

Thank you for choosing this coloring book!
Please consider leaving a positive review on
Amazon. It would mean a lot to me and help
other customers find the book.
Your feedback is greatly appreciated!

⭐ ⭐ ⭐ ⭐ ⭐

🖤 **Get Free Printable Coloring Pages** 🖤
& Join Our Community!

https://linktr.ee/5ideas.publishing

- MAXIMUS PRIME -

THANK YOU!

THANK YOU FOR CHOOSING US
TRY OUR OTHER COLORING BOOKS ON AMAZON
- MAXIMUS PRIME COLORING BOOKS-

Made in the USA
Las Vegas, NV
29 November 2024

12925694R00046